THE SPIRIT OF

NEWCASTLE

TONY HOPKINS

HALSGROVE

First published in Great Britain in 2007

British Library Cataloguing-in-Publication Data
A CIP record for this title is available from the British Library

ISBN 978 1 84114 665 2

HALSGROVE
Halsgrove House
Ryelands Farm Industrial Estate, Bagley Green,
Wellington, Somerset TA21 9PZ
Tel: 01823 653777 Fax: 01823 216796
email: sales@halsgrove.com
website: www.halsgrove.com

Printed and bound by D'Auria Industrie Grafiche, Italy

Introduction

This really is a city of all ages. But not just one city, nor one community. Separate until 1974, Newcastle and Gateshead are today united in the Metropolitan County of Tyne and Wear.

Newcastle has been a vibrant and vital settlement at least since Roman times. Shipbuilding and coal brought prosperity and expansion, and while the riverside was dirty and smelly, bustling and brash, the civic heart of the city centred on the elegant sweep of Grey Street and Grainger Town.

The mixture of grand buildings, green space, historic pubs and churches, a great river and a maritime outlook, help to give Newcastle/Gateshead a unique character. A revitalised Quayside has made the place the hub of contemporary art and music, and a successful football team, two universities and a thousand clubs and restaurants have kept its atmosphere lively and colourful, day and night.

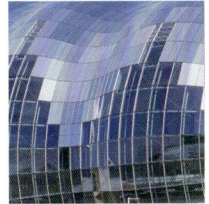

West from Swan Hunters' shipyards, with the ruins and rebuilt bathhouse of *Segedunum* Roman Fort. The river is wide and deep only because of extensive dredging in the mid-nineteenth century.

The Tyne on one of its showpiece days, the University Boat Race, with crowds gathered along the Quayside and on the Millennium Bridge. The race takes place every May between local rivals Durham and Newcastle. Durham usually wins.

Looking across the still waters of the Tyne to the Gateshead shore. The square building beside the river is the Baltic, once a derelict warehouse but now the Centre for Contemporary Arts. Beyond this, in the middle of the picture, is the curved glass dome of the Sage, the new centre for music in the region.

Scudding clouds on a bright March morning. The Millennium Bridge, a unique and elegant footbridge designed to tilt as ships pass beneath, is known locally as the Blinking Eye.

A summer evening, upstream from the Quayside,
with the city's bridges a jumble of coloured lights.

Opposite: A spring morning, looking west from the Gateshead side of
the Tyne Bridge over the Swing Bridge to the Guildhall and Sandhill.

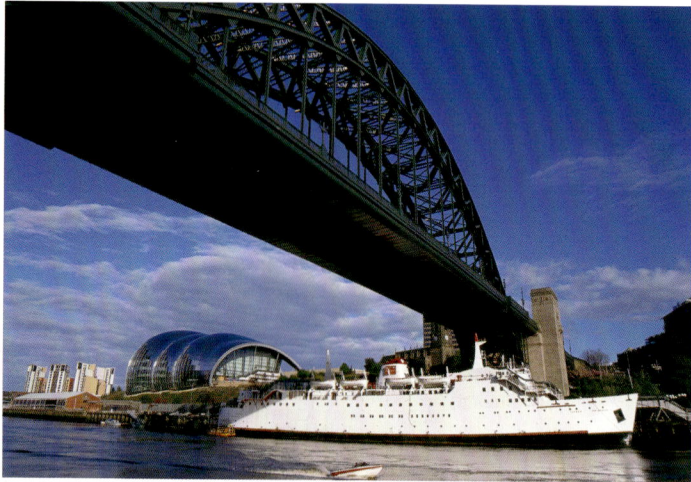

The Tyne was one of the busiest working waterways in Europe when
coal was king. The ship moored beneath the Tyne Bridge is the
Tuxedo Princess – a floating night-club.

Beneath the High Level Bridge, very early on a spring morning.

The very *art nouveau* Bridge Hotel,
in the shadow of the High Level Bridge.

Redheugh Bridge, on the riverside walkway at Skinnerburn Road.
The other six Tyne bridges are visible downstream.

The Copthorne Hotel, a pleasant stroll along the riverside
and a popular lunch-time venue for live music.

A cold morning across the rooftops, towards the Guildhall and the river.

Plaque beneath one of the upper windows of Bessie Surtees House on Sandhill. Proof that rich merchants' daughters were as brave as they were foolhardy.

Opposite:
Timber-framed frontage at Bessie Surtees House.

FROM THE ABOVE WINDOW
ON NOV 18TH 1772
BESSY SURTEES DESCENDED AND ELOPED WITH
JOHN SCOTT LATER CREATED 1ST EARL OF ELDON
AND LORD CHANCELLOR OF ENGLAND

Blackfriars – a cloister surviving from a medieval Dominican friary – founded in 1239 on a site beside the City Walls. The old refectory is now a coffee shop, and the grassy square is one of the best places to sit for a few minutes to escape the city's bustle.

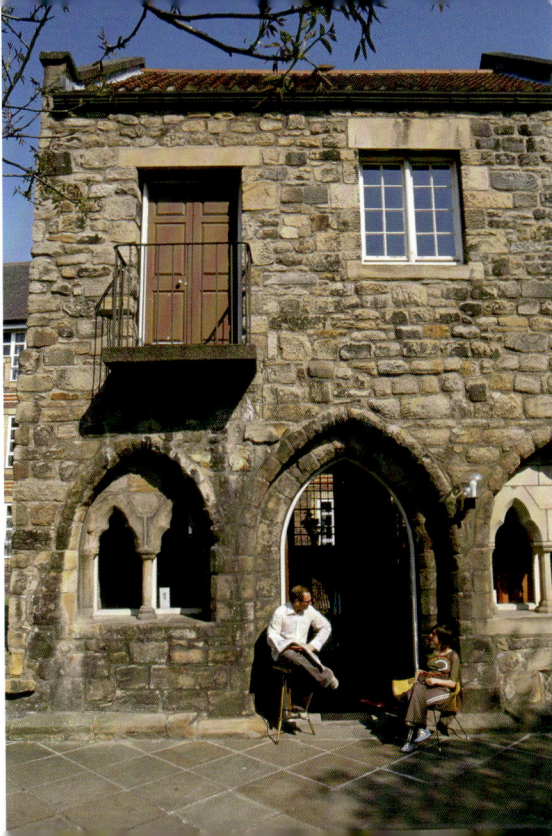

The buildings around Blackfriars cloister-yard were bought by the city corporation after the Dissolution in 1544, then leased to guilds or 'mysteries' ('Skinners and Glovers', 'Tanners and Tailors' etc). In the last few years, Blackfriars has been renovated and the buildings leased again to local crafts and boutiques.

19

The Castle Keep and Black Gate. A wooden castle was built on a motte (mound) on this site in 1080 by Robert, son of William the Conqueror.

Secret stonework
and suspended
doorways at
the Black Gate.

Queen Victoria,
dozing in
St Nicholas' Square.

A demonic rabbit crouches above a doorway into Cathedral Buildings, at Amen Corner, close to the site of Thomas Bewick's workshop at the back of St Nicholas' Cathedral.

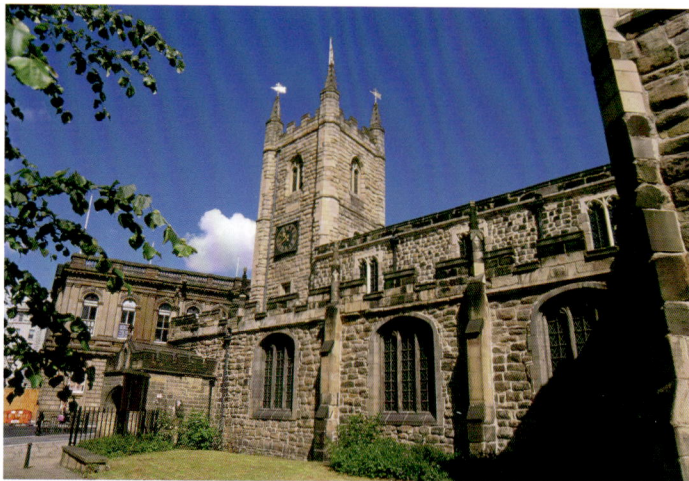

St John's church on Grainger Street, one of the prettiest and most compact of the city's medieval churches.

The Bishop's House – East Denton Hall – on the West Road.
An impressive Elizabethan mansion, built in the reign of James I and
(according to local legend) haunted by a particularly nasty ghost.

The Sallyport Gate, last of the surviving town gateways, positioned where the City Walls cross the line of Hadrian's Wall. The Sallyport was rebuilt in 1716 by the Company of Ships' Carpenters to serve as their meeting-hall.

Newcastle Opera House, one of the most imposing and valued of music venues
(for all sorts of music), but with a troubled history and often under new management.

Kings Walk and the gateway
to the University Quadrangle.
Newcastle is home to two
universities – Newcastle and
Northumbria – and the
walkways and cafés are often
awash with young people
clutching writing pads
and bottles of mineral water.

In the Quadrangle of the University of Newcastle. A few yards away
are the entrances to the Hutton Gallery and the Museum of Antiquities.

'Classical Newcastle', the core of the city now known as Grainger Town, was created around the 1830s by a group of architects and entrepreneurs led by Richard Grainger and John Dobson. Grey Street is a typically grand example of their work and the Theatre Royal is one of its most dramatic buildings.

Opposite:
Grey Street from the Grey Monument. A graceful curve of warm sandstone façades and Corinthian columns.

The Grey Monument, Monument Metro Station and Monument Mall. The raised 'stage' at the foot of the column is often used for live music events and speeches, and as the rallying point for protest marches: a mixture of Hyde Park and Trafalgar Square.

Earl Grey was a local hero turned Prime Minister, commemorated here not for his taste in tea but for his Reform Bill of 1832. The statue was the work of Edward Baily, who also created Nelson on his column in Trafalgar Square.

The 1960s, the era of T. Dan Smith, left several scars but few enduring landmarks in Newcastle. The Civic Centre, in the Haymarket, is an exception. The distinctive tower is crowned with a circle of twelve seahorse heads.

Vane Park in Jesmond:
exclusive flats
in one of the best
parts of town.

A new venue to meet, eat and see the latest film releases: The Gate on Newgate Street.

The Central Arcade,
between Grey Street and
Grainger Street.
The atmosphere is often
of sepulchral calm,
despite the regular
presence of buskers
(who are usually talented
students practising
their instruments).

Street or barrow-traders are the life and soul
of any city. Albert Sayer's family has been in
the business for three centuries and his stall on
Northumberland Street always does brisk business.

Opposite:
Northumberland Street, one of the busiest pedestrian
thoroughfares in Newcastle, on a midsummer morning.

The past, present and future of your life, told by a Welsh gypsy on Bigg Market.

Stowell Street in Chinatown: vibrant and colourful.
The restaurants back onto a well-preserved section of the Town Walls.

St James' Park football stadium, the home of Newcastle United FC, dominates the skyline just as the team is the main topic of conversation in the streets and pubs.

The quieter side of St James' Park: mute swans in Leazes Park.

The Sailors' Bethel, above Sandgate and the Quayside. This sailors' chapel was built in 1877 (to replace an older structure), and like many of Newcastle's historic buildings, it is now used as offices.

Formal borders and the Almond Pavillion:
civic pride on show at Saltwell Park in Gateshead.

Still waters in the heart of the city, at Leazes Park. The lake has been stocked with some impressive and elusive fish, especially carp.

Pets' Corner in Jesmond Dene, where local people
get to know local goats, chickens and other characters.

The Ouse Burn, looking north from Byker Bank. This area of the city, once known for its innovative craft industries, is now being revitalised as a creative business area.

Each summer, Town Moor hosts The Hoppings, billed as the biggest
travelling fair in Europe. It began as a temperance festival in 1882.

The Western Bypass (A1) and slip-road
for Gateshead and the Angel of the North.

Opposite:
A lay-by on the A167 allows easy access to visit
Antony Gormley's towering Angel of the North.

Spheres, the work of Richard Cole, along the riverside near Amethyst Road.
Across the Tyne are Dunston Coal Staithes.

Waiting for a bus at Gateshead Interchange. A public work of art by Danny Lane called Opening Line runs between the platforms.

Steel-blue sky mirrored
in the roof of The Sage
at Gateshead. The new
concert hall and complex
caters for all kinds of music,
from Northern Sinfonia
to Folkworks.

Opposite:
Unreal city:
Millennium and Sage,
like a futuristic Venice.

The Baltic: a big space for big ideas in art.
The Centre for Contemporary Arts houses four main galleries.
There are no permanent exhibitions: everything changes.

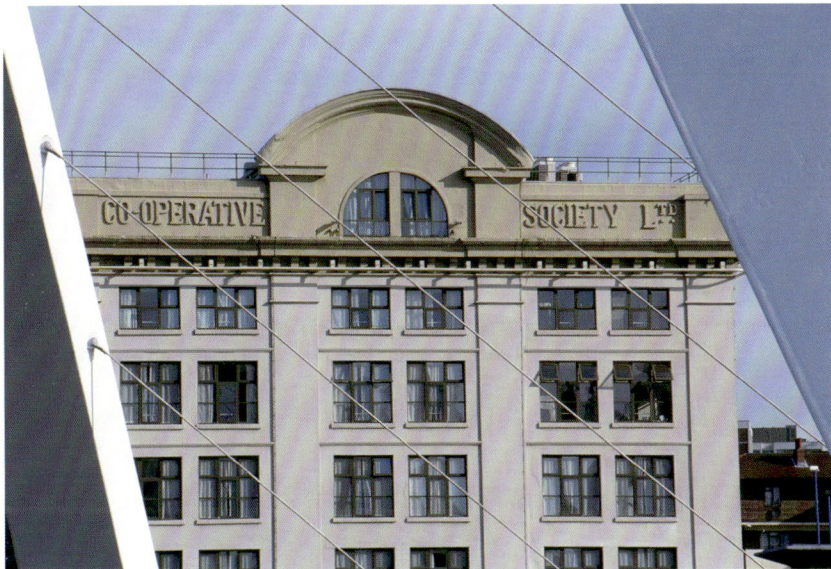

The Co-operative Society Warehouse on the Quayside is probably the oldest ferro-concrete building in the country. It suits its location well and looks surprisingly comfortable among more modern Quayside architecture.

Ex-smokers of a certain age will recognise the Wills Cigarette Factory,
on the Coast Road (A1058). An image of it appeared for
many years on packets of Woodbine cigarettes.

Newcastle Central Station: a curve of the track away
from the King Edward's Bridge, to the lower left.

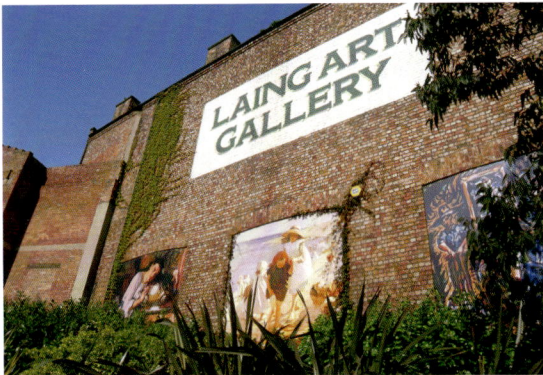

The Laing Art Gallery was built as an extension to the City Library in 1884. The library has since been demolished to make way for John Dobson Street, but the famous gallery remains.

Opposite:
North-east from Whickham Thorns, across the Western Bypass and the Tyne to the heart of the city.

The Life Science Centre, in Times Square, runs events and exhibitions explaining the origins of life. The emphasis is on making science fun for young people.

The glory of Classical
Newcastle: from Grey Street
to the Castle Keep and
High Level Bridge.

Tyne Bridge by night. Time to party.